# This Book Belongs To........

..................................................................

..................................................................

..................................................................

..................................................................

Made in the USA
Monee, IL
11 March 2022

92701599R10063